TRUCKS

CHRIS OXLADE

A⁺
Smart Apple Media

Published by Smart Apple Media
2140 Howard Drive West, North Mankato, Minnesota 56003

Created by Q2A Creative, Editor: Chester Fisher, Designers: Mini Dhawan, Ashita Murgai
Picture Researcher: Simmi Sikka, Somnath Bowmick

Picture Credits
Aam Alberti: 21t, Amdac-Carmichael Limited: 20t, American LaFrance: 20b,
Atkins-Racing: 25t, Daimler Chrysler: 6t, 11b,
Elgin Sweeper Company—A subsidiary of Federal Signal Corporation: 12t,
Fassi Group: 17b, Ford: 22b, Freight Liner: Cover, Fuso Truck and Bus Corporation: 28c,
General Motors: 22t, 29t, Jason Ellis: 25b, Kenworth Truck Company, a Division of PACCAR: 4b, 9b,
Liebherr Mining Equipment Co.: 26b, Mack Trucks, Inc.: 11t, 14t,
Oshkosh Truck Corporation: 12b, 13t, 18t, 19t, 29b, Scania Trucks: 4t, 5b, 7t, 7b, 9t, 15b, 31t,
Sterling Trucks: 21b, Steve Huddy: 8b, Tadano Faun: 16b, 17t,
Volvo: 6b, 10b, Wecar Trucks and Technology: 19b, Western Star Trucks: 27b,
www.travel-images.com: 27t.

Printed in United States

Oct. 2008
8/8 95)

Library of Congress Cataloging-in-Publication Data
Oxlade, Chris
Trucks / by Chris Oxlade
p. cm. — (Mighty machines)
Includes index.
ISBN-13: 978-1-58340-920-6
1. Trucks—Juvenile literature. I. Title. II. Series.

TL230.15.O95 2006
629.224—dc22   2006002933

4 6 8 9 7 5 3

CONTENTS

MIGHTY TRUCKS

Trucks are the mightiest machines on the road. Trucks carry all sorts of cargo, from packages to gasoline, but they also put out fires, lift loads, fight battles, and mix concrete.

TYPES OF TRUCKS

Trucks do dozens of different jobs for us, but there are only two main types of trucks: articulated trucks and rigid trucks (see below). An articulated truck is made up of a tractor unit and a semitrailer. The semitrailer carries the cargo.

Sleeping compartment
Contains a bunk and sink

Cab
Contains driving controls

Trailer attachment
Also called the "fifth wheel"

Engine compartment
Contains engine and other parts

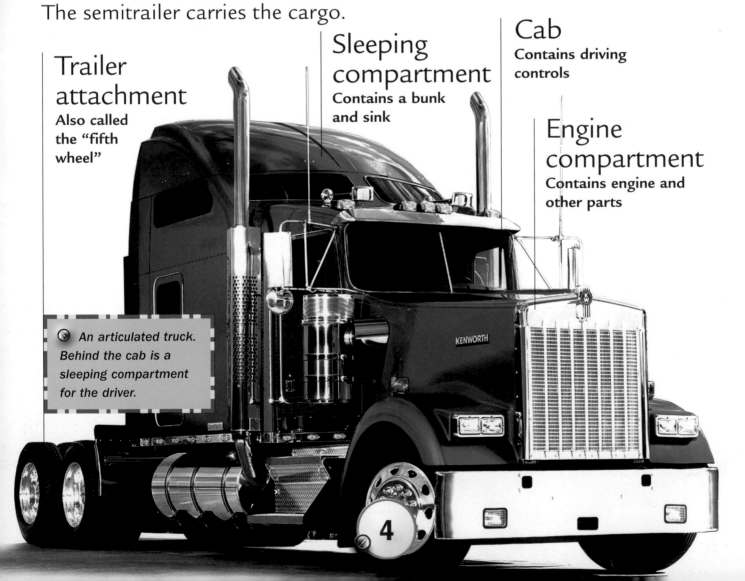

An articulated truck. Behind the cab is a sleeping compartment for the driver.

KENWORTH

4

Pickup truck

Fire truck

Tanker

Road-train

⊙ Small trucks have rigid bodies. Large trucks are articulated so that they can turn corners more easily.

---- FAST FACTS
Trailer Pickup
To pick up a semitrailer, a driver backs the tractor unit underneath its front. A large pin on the trailer automatically slides into a hole on the tractor.

RIGID TRUCKS

Small trucks do not need to be articulated. They only need two front wheels, so they can go around corners without needing to bend in the middle. All rigid trucks have a rigid chassis with a cab for the driver at the front. Any sort of body, from a simple box for cargo to a complex cement mixer, can be built on the back.

Air deflector
Deflects air over the body

Rear wheels
Turned by the engine

Chassis
Made from strong steel

Small cab
Contains driving controls but no sleeping compartment

⊙ The chassis of a rigid truck. It contains the engine, wheels, and cab. It is ready for a body to be added.

HOW TRUCKS WORK

All trucks, big or small, work in a similar way. They have large wheels and tires to carry heavy loads, a powerful engine, plenty of gears, and air-powered brakes.

UNDER THE HOOD

There are two kinds of truck cabs: conventional and cabover. In a conventional truck, the engine is in front of the cab under a long hood. In a cabover cab, the engine is under the cab. This makes the cab shorter and gives more space behind it for cargo.

⊙ In a cabover truck, the whole cab tilts forward so mechanics can service and repair the engine.

Transmission
Connects the engine to the wheels

Engine
Drives the truck

Fuel tank
Contains enough fuel to drive hundreds of miles

⊙ A conventional truck. A shaft that turns the rear wheels goes under the cab.

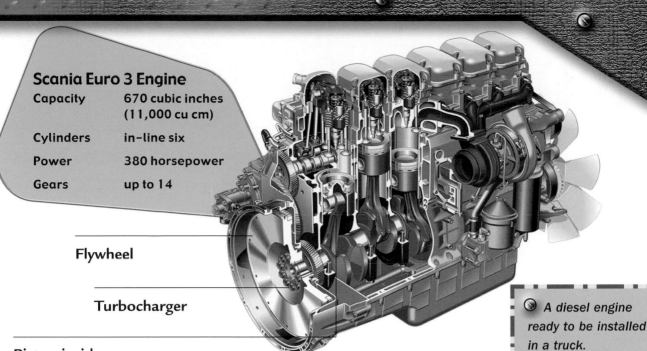

Scania Euro 3 Engine

Capacity	670 cubic inches (11,000 cu cm)
Cylinders	in-line six
Power	380 horsepower
Gears	up to 14

Flywheel

Turbocharger

Piston inside cylinder

A diesel engine ready to be installed in a truck.

----- FAST FACTS

Mighty Engines

A truck engine is 10 times as big as a family car engine, and it has 10 times the power. It weighs the same as the car, too!

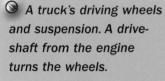

A truck's driving wheels and suspension. A drive-shaft from the engine turns the wheels.

ENGINES AND GEARS

Almost all trucks are powered by a powerful diesel engine. A big engine has a capacity of 974 cubic inches (16 l) or more, giving plenty of power to pull 44–55 tons (40–50 t) of cargo. Truck engines have turbochargers that pump air into the cylinders. This allows extra fuel to be burned for extra power. Trucks can have 18 or more gears—low ones for starting off and going uphill, and high ones for road cruising.

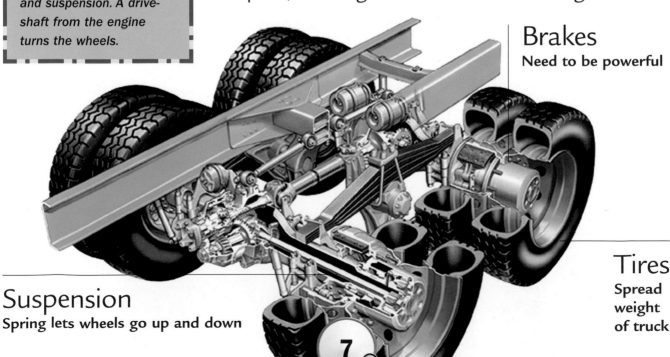

Brakes
Need to be powerful

Tires
Spread weight of truck

Suspension
Spring lets wheels go up and down

MIGHTY TRUCKS

7

EARLY TRUCKS

Before trucks were invented, more cargo was carried by boats and trains than on the roads. Things changed in the 1800s, when steam engines began to replace horses for pulling wagons.

Cargo
Carried on flatbed

Funnel
Carries away smoke and steam

A steam truck built in Britain in the 1920s by the Foden company.

STEAM TRUCKS

The first trucks were built in the mid-1800s. They were powered by steam engines. In a steam engine, burning coal heated water, which boiled to make steam. The steam was fed to cylinders and made pistons move in and out of them to turn the wheels. Diesel and gas engines were invented in the 1890s, but steam trucks were still in use until the 1920s.

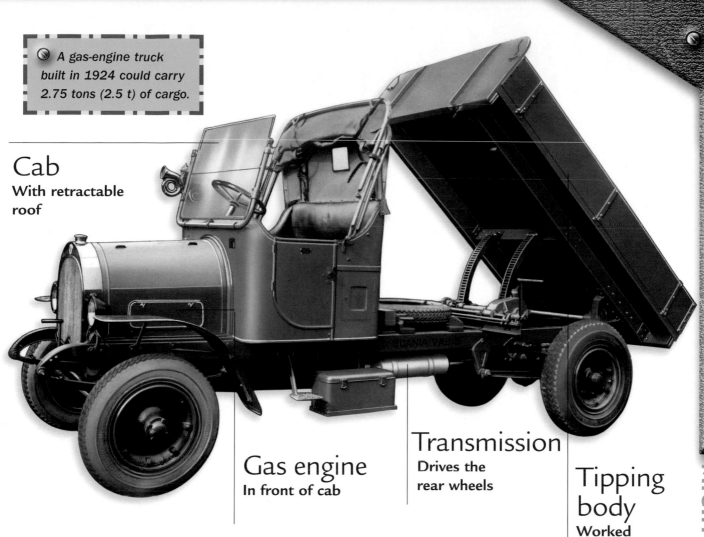

A gas-engine truck built in 1924 could carry 2.75 tons (2.5 t) of cargo.

Cab
With retractable roof

Gas engine
In front of cab

Transmission
Drives the rear wheels

Tipping body
Worked by hand

DIESEL DOMINATES

By the 1930s, trucks with gas engines and diesel engines had taken over from trucks with steam engines. By the 1940s, however, most trucks were using diesel engines because they were cheaper to run than gas engines.

---- FAST FACTS
The First Truck
The first successful steam-powered vehicle was built in 1769 by a French military engineer named Nicolas Cugnot. It was designed to tow large guns.

The Kenworth truck was designed to be able to lug a large quantity of cargo within an economically constructed space.

9

CARGO TRUCKS

The bodies of trucks are made in dozens of different shapes and sizes to carry all sorts of cargo.

TANKERS

Trucks with tanker bodies carry liquids such as oil, water, and milk. The tank is in the shape of a cylinder, which makes it strong and also easy to make. Valves on top and at the rear are used for filling and emptying the tank. Bulk carriers are similar to tankers, but they carry powders, such as cement and flour, instead.

Tank
Made from aluminum or steel

Hazard sign
Shows contents of tanker

A tanker truck with two trailers. Each holds about 5,800 gallons (22,000 l) of liquid.

Trailers that sit very close to the ground are designed to carry heavy vehicles such as diggers and tanks.

Low trailer
Allows vehicles to drive on and off

BODY STYLES

The most common truck bodies are flatbed bodies, box bodies, and bodies with flexible, removable sides. Flatbed bodies carry large loads that are lifted on and off by crane. Box bodies can be refrigerated, so they can carry cargo such as frozen foods. Cargo is tied down to keep it from sliding around.

A tractor-and-box-body semitrailer. The trailer's body has a simple frame covered with aluminum panels.

SPECIAL JOBS

Many types of trucks don't carry cargo at all. Instead, their bodies have equipment mounted on them to do specialized jobs around towns, cities, and airports.

UTILITY TRUCKS

Local authorities use several types of utility trucks. These are trucks built to do a special job. Garbage trucks move through the streets collecting garbage from houses, factories, schools, and stores. Sweeper trucks keep gutters clear, while snowplows and salt spreaders keep roads safe when there is snow and ice.

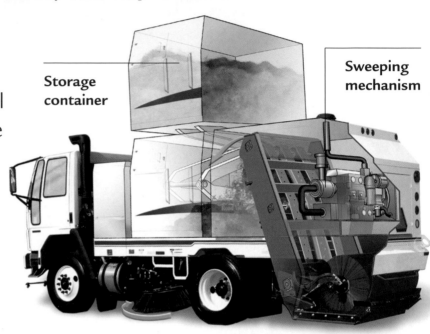

Storage container

Sweeping mechanism

Body
Stores crushed garbage

⊘ *A garbage truck lifts up garbage cans, tips the garbage into the truck, and crushes it into a small space.*

Cab
For driver and crew

Garbage Can
Tipped by mechanism

Blade
Spins to collect snow

This snowplow collects snow with a blade and blows it away to the roadside through a chute.

AIRPORT TRUCKS

Busy airports have trucks that do lots of different jobs, such as servicing aircraft and keeping the runways open. Refueling tankers keep aircraft fuel tanks full. Aircraft tractors are the most specialized airport trucks. They push and pull heavy aircraft around the tarmac.

FAST FACTS
Always Ready
Airport fire trucks are always on standby when aircraft are taking off and landing so that they can attend to any emergency immediately.

An aircraft tractor sits close to the ground so that it can fit under the nose of an aircraft to hold on to the nose undercarriage.

SUPER MOVERS

Trucks are always on the move on construction sites. They move earth and rubble from place to place and mix and pump concrete.

> ◉ A concrete mixer has a motor that turns the drum. It can carry several tons of concrete.

Chute
Unfolds to deliver concrete

Drum
Spins to mix concrete

CONCRETE MIXERS

A concrete mixing truck is a giant mixer on wheels. It starts its journey at a concrete factory, where the ingredients of the concrete (cement, sand, gravel, and water) are poured into its drum. At the building site, the drum slowly turns, mixing the ingredients together.

> ◉ A concrete pump is a truck that pumps fresh, runny concrete through pipes to where it is needed.

Boom

Delivery pipe

Stabilizers

DUMP TRUCKS

Dump trucks move earth and rubble around building sites. They also work in quarries and mines. They have super-strong, open-topped bodies that are tipped up by hydraulic rams to pour their contents onto the ground. Dump trucks have large wheels with chunky tires to keep them from sinking or slipping on muddy ground.

---- FAST FACTS

Concrete Carrier

A large concrete mixer can carry as much as 15 bathtubs worth of concrete, weighing about 33 tons (30 t).

Cab
Contains controls for dump truck

Hydraulic ram
Pushes body up to empty

Gate
Opens to let gravel pour out

A dump truck on a Scania truck chassis. The dump truck body and mechanism have been added to the chassis.

15

MOBILE CRANES

A mobile crane is a crane mounted on top of a truck. The crane's arm folds away when the crane is driving along the road. It extends when the crane reaches the site.

MULTI-TERRAIN CRANE

The biggest mobile cranes are giant machines. Their crane arms are called booms and can reach high up into the air or extend far over the truck. These trucks are multi-terrain vehicles. They can cross bumpy, muddy building sites as well as drive on roads. Mobile cranes are used to lift and move exceptionally heavy loads, such as concrete beams for bridges.

Hydraulic ram
Lifts boom into the air

A large multi-terrain crane with a telescopic boom. Each section of the boom slides inside the next.

16

Crane boom
Folded away while on road

Faun ATE 65G-4

Weight	53 tons (48 t)
Maximum reach	145 feet (44 m)
Maximum load	72 tons (65 t)
Top speed	53 miles (85 km) per hour

Cab
Crane operator sits here

> When the boom of a crane is extended, stabilizers are lowered to keep the crane from tipping over.

Wheels
Each wheel has its own suspension

> A flatbed truck loading building materials with the grappling hook on its onboard crane.

ONBOARD CRANES

Many flatbed trucks have onboard cranes for loading and unloading cargo. The cranes lift materials from the truck onto the ground. These trucks are also called boom trucks.

FAST FACTS

Tallest Cranes

The biggest mobile cranes have booms that can reach more than 330 feet (100 m) into the air. That's long enough to reach the 25th floor of an office building!

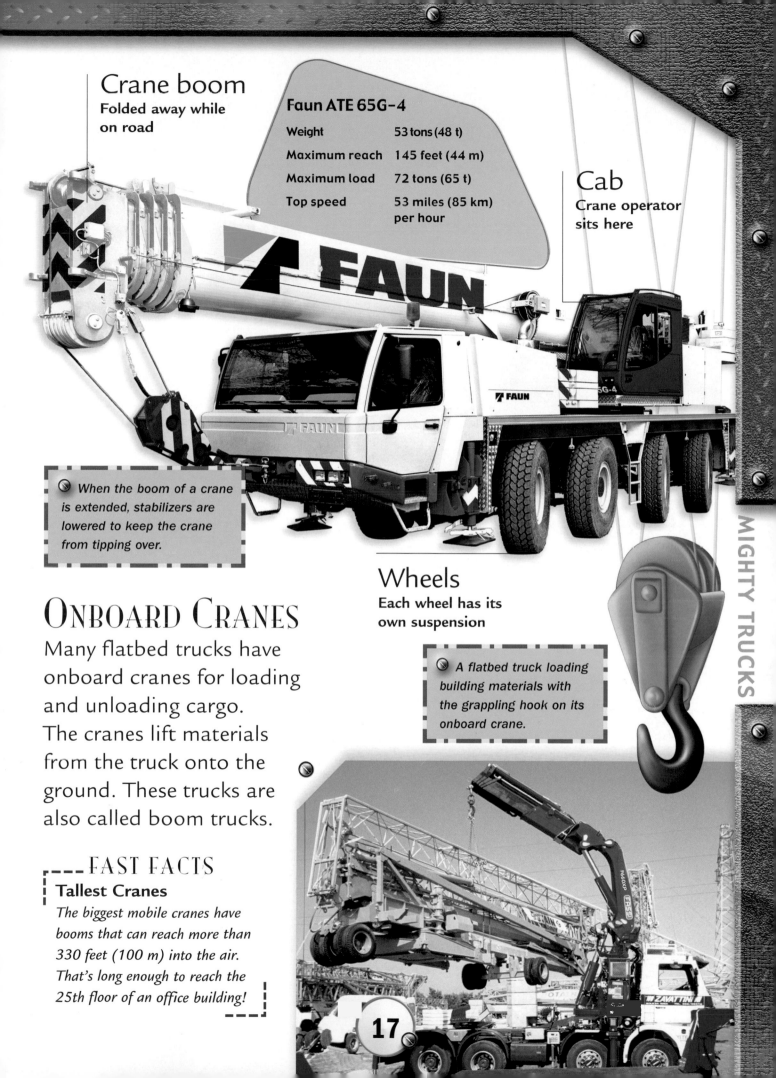

17

MILITARY TRUCKS

Armies use trucks for all sorts of things, such as transporting troops, equipment, and supplies to the battlefield, and for helping in rescues after natural disasters.

The Oshkosh PLS off-road truck has a powered hook that loads and unloads equipment from its body.

Armored front
Protects engine from rocks

Pallet
Changeable pallet for load

Wheels
All wheels are turned by the engine

Chunky tires
Give grip in the mud

OFF-ROAD WORKERS

Military trucks often need to travel where other trucks can't go—along rough tracks and across fields, deserts, and snow. To do this, the engine drives all of the wheels (this is called all-wheel drive). The wheels are large, and the suspension is high. These features give lots of grip and space under the chassis for going over bumps.

A general-purpose military truck. It can tow trailers and guns as well as carry cargo.

FAST FACTS
Beach Landers
Amphibious vehicles are also used to land troops and equipment on beaches. They drive through the water from landing craft to the beach.

Radiator
Cools large, powerful diesel engine

AMPHIBIANS

Rivers are big obstacles for armies on the move. Some army trucks are amphibious. This means that they can drive on land like trucks, but they can also float in the water. Underneath, the chassis is sealed tight to keep water from getting in.

Bison Amphibious Truck

Weight	12 tons (11 t)
Engine	V8 supercharged diesel
Wheels	4 x 4
Maximum speed (land)	60 miles (100 km) per hour
Maximum speed (water)	6 miles (10 km) per hour

The Bison amphibious truck has inflatable floats to keep it stable in the water.

MIGHTY TRUCKS

EMERGENCY!

Fire and rescue trucks are used by emergency services to fight fires, rescue people trapped in cars and buildings, and recover vehicles.

Water pump

Operator platform
for directing operations

The Cobra 2 fire rescue vehicle has six-wheel drive and water and foam tanks.

Equipment lockers

Cobra 2

Length	38 feet (11.5 m)
Power	700 horsepower
Water	2,640 gallons (10,000 l)
Foam	370 gallons (1,400 l)

FIRE TRUCKS

There are three main types of fire trucks—ladder trucks, water tenders, and airport fire trucks. Ladder trucks have extending ladders that reach high into the air. Water tenders are general-purpose firefighting vehicles.

The ladder of a ladder truck extends to reach the upper floors of buildings. Firefighters work from the platform on the end of the ladder.

Large cab
With seats for crew

Lockers
For fire equipment

A fire department rescue truck at the scene of an accident.

Tow Trucks

A tow truck is designed to rescue broken-down cars, buses, and other trucks. Small tow trucks can carry or tow a car. The biggest tow trucks can tow double-decker buses and big trucks. They have powerful hooks that pick up the front of the broken-down vehicle to pull it along. They also have winches to pull vehicles from ditches.

FAST FACTS

Power Pumps

Fire trucks have powerful water pumps for spraying water. A typical pump can pour out 2,115 gallons (8,000 l) of water a minute. That's a bathtub-full every 10 seconds!

A heavy-duty tow truck for recovering broken-down and damaged trucks and buses.

MIGHTY TRUCKS

CUSTOM TRUCKS

Truck enthusiasts like to customize their trucks. They add new parts to the truck bodies, make engines more powerful, and paint the bodies with interesting artwork.

CUSTOM PICKUPS

Pickup trucks are the smallest trucks. They are also the trucks that are most customized. Their owners add engine parts such as superchargers for extra power, wide wheels with big tires, and high suspensions to lift the trucks high off the ground.

Customized pickup trucks like this race in the NASCAR truck series.

Roll cage
Protects driver in an accident

Body shell
Aerodynamically shaped for speed

Cab
Leather seats can be added at the factory

The Ford F-150 pickup truck can be customized by adding extra parts at the factory.

CUSTOM RIGS

"Rig" is the nickname for a truck or tractor unit. Some owners customize their rigs in the same way that pickup owners do. They paint the cabs, add colored lights and chrome parts, and keep the bodywork in perfect condition. Enthusiasts enter their trucks into competitions for the best custom rigs.

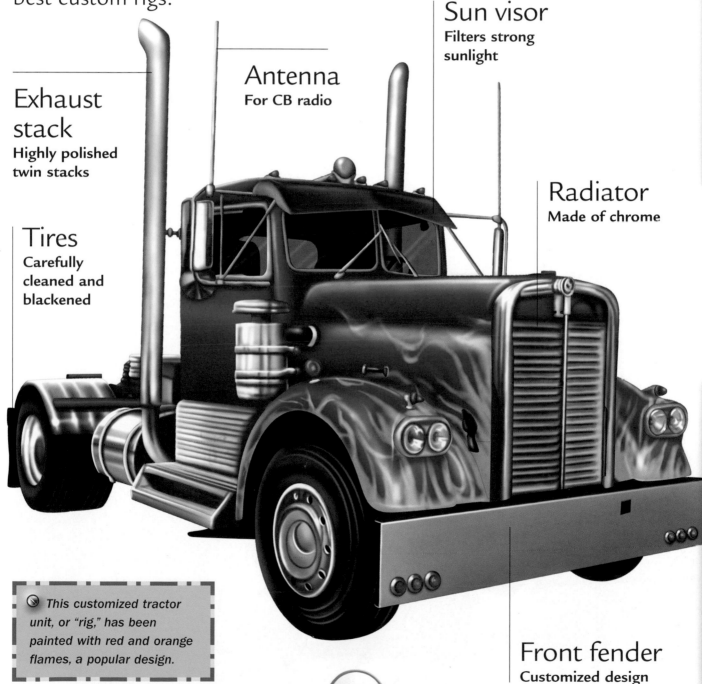

Sun visor
Filters strong sunlight

Antenna
For CB radio

Exhaust stack
Highly polished twin stacks

Radiator
Made of chrome

Tires
Carefully cleaned and blackened

This customized tractor unit, or "rig," has been painted with red and orange flames, a popular design.

Front fender
Customized design

TRUCK SPORTS

Truck racing is a popular sport. Trucks race each other around racetracks and side by side around drag–racing tracks.

MONSTER TRUCKS

Monster trucks are amazing customized pickup trucks with giant wheels and tires normally used on dump trucks. They also have super-powerful turbocharged engines and special suspensions that lift them high into the air. Monster trucks race each other around obstacle courses, jumping high over dirt ramps and piles of old, squashed cars.

Bodywork
Painted and polished

Monster trucks always feature huge, outsized suspensions, wheels, and tires, and a custom chassis and paintwork.

High suspension
Lifts truck body above wheels

Dump truck wheels and tires
Let truck roll over giant obstacles

Truck racing is fast and furious. Trucks often collide as they try to pass.

Engine
Standard engine with turbocharger

MAN Race Truck	
Engine	6-cylinder turbo diesel
Power	1,050 horsepower
Weight	13.8 tons (12.5 t)
Maximum speed	100 miles (160 km) per hour

TRUCKS ON TRACK

In another form of truck racing, the tractor units of articulated trucks are raced around tracks. There are local, national, and international truck-racing championships. The trucks look like normal tractor units, with much more powerful engines and features such as racing tires, brakes, and suspensions.

FAST FACTS
Truck vs. Car
A racing tractor unit has an engine 20 times more powerful than a family car. It could leave the car in the dust in a race!

Drag-racing pickup trucks race head-to-head on a short, straight track.

EXTREME TRUCKS

Here you can discover some of the world's heaviest, longest, and most powerful trucks.

GIANT DUMP TRUCKS

The giants of the truck world are the mega-dump trucks that work in quarries and surface mines. They carry huge loads of earth, rock, and rubble. These monsters are the heaviest and tallest trucks. Their engines drive generators that produce electricity, which powers electric motors that drive the wheels.

Driver's cab
Reached by ladder from the ground

The Liebherr T 282B is the world's heaviest truck fully loaded.

Liebherr T 282B

Weight	353 tons (320 t)
Power	3,618 horsepower
Maximum load	397 tons (360 t)
Maximum speed	40 miles (65 km) per hour

Bed
Tips up to dump load

Tires
Each tire is taller than an adult

Semitrailers

Sleeper cab

A tanker road-train being pulled by a super-powerful tractor.

ROAD-TRAINS

Trucks often pull a trailer behind them, attached by a tow bar. A truck with two or more trailers is called a road-train because it is like a train locomotive that pulls lots of freight cars. Road-trains are popular in the Australian outback, where trucks travel with sheep, cattle, and other cargo.

Giant loads are pulled on trailers with dozens of wheels by super-powerful tractors.

Load
Bolted firmly to truck

Tractor unit
Stays in low gear to pull load

FUTURE TRUCKS

In the future, trucks will become even more efficient, using less fuel and making less pollution. They will use new technology but will probably not look much different from the trucks of today.

CONCEPT TRUCKS

A concept truck is an example of what truck manufacturers think their trucks might look like in a few years' time. Concept trucks feature interesting streamlined body shapes and new technologies that might be used in the future. Concept trucks are used to demonstrate new ideas.

All-glass cab
For good visibility

Bumper
Collapses safely in accident

Air deflector
For fuel economy

Video cameras
For all-around vision when turning and reversing

Low-resistance tires
For fuel economy

The Mitsubishi FUSO concept truck is designed to be safe for the driver and pedestrians, comfortable to drive, and environmentally friendly.

A General Motors military truck. It has a diesel engine and a fuel cell for power.

Antennas
For radio communications

Cargo area
For troops and equipment

SELF-DRIVING TRUCKS

Some manufacturers are experimenting with autonomous trucks. An autonomous vehicle is a vehicle that drives itself, so it doesn't need a human driver. It is remotely controlled by radio or is completely automatic. Autonomous trucks could be especially useful for armies. Then human drivers would not have to drive into dangerous situations.

FAST FACTS
Satellite Navigation
Autonomous trucks use the global positioning system (GPS) to find their way around.

A Terramax all-terrain autonomous military truck. There is no driver!

TIMELINE

1769
French engineer Nicolas Cugnot builds a steam tractor for pulling military guns, creating the world's first powered vehicle.

1802
In Britain, Richard Trevithick builds a steam carriage that travels on roads.

1804
The world's first amphibious vehicle is built in the U.S.

1831
The British government makes laws to keep steam-powered vehicles from using public roads because of safety fears.

1860
Frenchman Etienne Lenoir builds the first internal combustion engine.

1876
The first truck, a steam-powered machine weighing 4.4 tons (4 t), is built in Britain.

1885
Gottlieb Daimler builds the first gas-powered internal combustion engine.

1885
In Germany, Karl Benz builds the first motor car, using a gas-powered internal combustion engine.

1896
Daimler builds the first gas-powered truck.

1897
German engineer Rudolf Diesel demonstrates his diesel engine.

1898
The first articulated truck is made by the Thornycroft company.

1904
Power steering is introduced in trucks.

1907
The first truck show is held in Chicago.

1914
The first truck production line is started by the Ford company in the U.S.

1914–18
Trucks transport troops and equipment in World War I.

1920s
The cabover engine layout is developed, trucks begin using pneumatic tires, and the first six-wheel rigid trucks are built.

1930s
Manufacturers experiment with streamlined trucks.

1950s
Diesel engines become widely used in trucks.

1954
Volvo introduces turbocharged diesel engines.

2003
The world's longest road-train is put together in Australia.

GLOSSARY

amphibious

A truck that can work as a boat as well as move on land.

articulated truck

A truck made up of a tractor unit and a semitrailer, with a flexible joint between them.

cabover

A tractor unit or rigid truck with the cab over the top of the engine.

chassis

The solid frame of a tractor unit or rigid truck.

cylinder

A space inside an engine that a piston moves in and out of. Burning fuel or high-pressure steam pushes the piston out, making the engine work.

diesel engine

An internal combustion engine that uses diesel fuel and does not have spark plugs like a gas engine.

gas engine

An internal combustion engine that uses gas as fuel, which is ignited by electric spark plugs in the cylinders.

hydraulic

Describes a machine that has parts operated by liquid pushed along pipes.

internal combustion engine

An engine in which the fuel is burned inside the cylinders. Gas and diesel engines are internal combustion engines.

pneumatic tire

A tire that is filled with air. All modern vehicles have pneumatic tires, but the first trucks had solid rubber tires.

power steering

A steering system that uses some power from a truck's engine to make turning the steering wheel easier.

rigid truck

A truck with a single rigid chassis, with the cab and body built on top.

road-train

A truck made up of a tractor unit or rigid truck with two or more trailers towed behind.

streamlined

With a smooth shape that moves easily through the air.

supercharger

A device that pumps air into an engine, allowing more fuel to be burned, and thereby improving power.

suspension

A system of springs and dampers that allow a truck's wheels to move up and down over bumps.

tractor

The front part of an articulated truck, containing the engine, cab, and driving wheels.

turbocharger

A device that pumps air into an engine, allowing more fuel to be burned and thus improving power. It is powered by exhaust gases.

INDEX

WEB FINDER

http://www.worldfiretrucks.com *Hundreds of photographs of fire trucks.*

http://www.oshkoshtruck.com *Home page of Oshkosh trucks.*

http://trucktrend.com *Features on all types of trucks, past, present, and future.*

http://www.monstertruckracing.com *Photographs and information on monster truck racing.*

http://www.faun.de/index-e.htm *Web site of Faun mobile cranes.*

http://www.macktrucks.com *Official site of Mack, a large American truck builder.*

http://www.roadtrains.com.au *Site dedicated to giant road-trains. Lots of photographs.*

http://www.militarytrucks.man-mn.com/en/en.jsp *Lots of information about military trucks.*